Great Works

Instructional for **Literature**

M.C. Higgins, the Great

A guide for the novel by Virginia Hamilton
Great Works Author: Suzanne Barchers, Ed.D.

SHELL EDUCATION

Table of Contents

How to Use This Literature Guide (cont.)

Vocabulary

Each teacher overview page has definitions and sentences about how key vocabulary words are used in the section. These words should be introduced and discussed with students. There are two student vocabulary activity pages in each section. On the first page, students are asked to define the ten words chosen by the author of this unit. On the second page in most sections, each student will select at least eight words that he or she finds interesting or difficult. For each section, choose one of these pages for your students to complete. With either assignment, you may want to have students get into pairs to discuss the meanings of the words. Allow students to use reference guides to define the words. Monitor students to make sure the definitions they have found are accurate and relate to how the words are used in the text.

On some of the vocabulary student pages, students are asked to answer text-related questions about the vocabulary words. The following question stems will help you create your own vocabulary questions if you'd like to extend the discussion.

- How does this word describe _____'s character?
- In what ways does this word relate to the problem in this story?
- How does this word help you understand the setting?
- In what ways is this word related to the story's solution?
- Describe how this word supports the novel's theme of . . . .
- What visual images does this word bring to your mind?
- For what reasons might the author have chosen to use this particular word?

At times, more work with the words will help students understand their meanings. The following quick vocabulary activities are a good way to further study the words.

- Have students practice their vocabulary and writing skills by creating sentences and/or paragraphs in which multiple vocabulary words are used correctly and with evidence of understanding.
- Students can play vocabulary concentration. Students make a set of cards with the words and a separate set of cards with the definitions. Then, students lay the cards out on the table and play concentration. The goal of the game is to match vocabulary words with their definitions.
- Students can create word journal entries about the words. Students choose words they think are important and then describe why they think each word is important within the novel.

How to Use This Literature Guide (cont.)

Analyzing the Literature

After students have read each section, hold small-group or whole-class discussions. Questions are written at two levels of complexity to allow you to decide which questions best meet the needs of your students. The Level 1 questions are typically less abstract than the Level 2 questions. Level 1 is indicated by a square, while Level 2 is indicated by a triangle. These questions focus on the various story elements, such as character, setting, and plot. Student pages are provided if you want to assign these questions for individual student work before your group discussion. Be sure to add further questions as your students discuss what they've read. For each question, a few key points are provided for your reference as you discuss the novel with students.

Reader Response

In today's classrooms, there are often great readers who are below average writers. So much time and energy is spent in classrooms getting students to read on grade level, that little time is left to focus on writing skills. To help teachers include more writing in their daily literacy instruction, each section of this guide has a literature-based reader response prompt. Each of the three genres of writing is used in the reader responses within this guide: narrative, informative/explanatory, and argument. Students have a choice between two prompts for each reader response. One response requires students to make connections between the reading and their own lives. The other prompt requires students to determine text-to-text connections or connections within the text.

Close Reading the Literature

Within each section, students are asked to closely reread a short section of text. Since some versions of the novels have different page numbers, the selections are described by chapter and location, along with quotations to guide the readers. After each close reading, there are text-dependent questions to be answered by students.

Encourage students to read each question one at a time and then go back to the text and discover the answer. Work with students to ensure that they use the text to determine their answers rather than making unsupported inferences. Once students have answered the questions, discuss what they discovered. Suggested answers are provided in the answer key.

How to Use This Literature Guide (cont.)

Close Reading the Literature (cont.)

The generic, open-ended stems below can be used to write your own text-dependent questions if you would like to give students more practice.

- Give evidence from the text to support . . . .
- Justify your thinking using text evidence about . . . .
- Find evidence to support your conclusions about . . . .
- What text evidence helps the reader understand . . . ?
- Use the book to tell why _____ happens.
- Based on events in the story, ...
- Use text evidence to describe why . . . .

Making Connections

The activities in this section help students make cross-curricular connections to writing, mathematics, science, social studies, or the fine arts. Each of these types of activities requires higher-order thinking skills from students.

Creating with the Story Elements

It is important to spend time discussing the common story elements in literature. Understanding the characters, setting, and plot can increase students' comprehension and appreciation of the story. If teachers discuss these elements daily, students will more likely internalize the concepts and look for the elements in their independent reading. Another important reason for focusing on the story elements is that students will be better writers if they think about how the stories they read are constructed.

Students are given three options for working with the story elements. They are asked to create something related to the characters, setting, or plot of the novel. Students are given a choice on this activity so that they can decide to complete the activity that most appeals to them. Different multiple intelligences are used so that the activities are diverse and interesting to all students.

How to Use This Literature Guide (cont.)

Culminating Activity

This open-ended, cross-curricular activity requires higher-order thinking and allows for a creative product. Students will enjoy getting the chance to share what they have discovered through reading the novel. Be sure to allow them enough time to complete the activity at school or home.

Comprehension Assessment

The questions in this section are modeled after current standardized tests to help students analyze what they've read and prepare for tests they may see in their classrooms. The questions are dependent on the text and require critical-thinking skills to answer.

Response to Literature

The final post-reading activity is an essay based on the text that also requires further research by students. This is a great way to extend this book into other curricular areas. A suggested rubric is provided for teacher reference.

Correlation to the Standards

Shell Education is committed to producing educational materials that are research and standards based. As part of this effort, we have correlated all of our products to the academic standards of all 50 states, the District of Columbia, the Department of Defense Dependents Schools, and all Canadian provinces.

Purpose and Intent of Standards

Standards are designed to focus instruction and guide adoption of curricula. Standards are statements that describe the criteria necessary for students to meet specific academic goals. They define the knowledge, skills, and content students should acquire at each level. Standards are also used to develop standardized tests to evaluate students' academic progress. Teachers are required to demonstrate how their lessons meet standards. Standards are used in the development of all of our products, so educators can be assured they meet high academic standards.

How to Find Standards Correlations

To print a customized correlation report of this product for your state, visit our website at http://www.shelleducation.com and follow the online directions. If you require assistance in printing correlation reports, please contact our Customer Service Department at 1-877-777-3450.

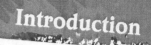

Correlation to the Standards (cont.)

Standards Correlation Chart

The lessons in this guide were written to support the Common Core College and Career Readiness Anchor Standards. This chart indicates which sections of this guide address the anchor standards.

Common Core College and Career Readiness Anchor Standard	Section
CCSS.ELA-Literacy.CCRA.R.1—Read closely to determine what the text says explicitly and to make logical inferences from it; cite specific textual evidence when writing or speaking to support conclusions drawn from the text.	Close Reading the Literature Sections 1–5; Analyzing the Literature Sections 1–5
CCSS.ELA-Literacy.CCRA.R.2—Determine central ideas or themes of a text and analyze their development; summarize the key supporting details and ideas.	Analyzing the Literature Sections 1–5; Creating with the Story Elements Sections 1–5
CCSS.ELA-Literacy.CCRA.R.3—Analyze how and why individuals, events, or ideas develop and interact over the course of a text.	Analyzing the Literature Sections 1–5; Creating with the Story Elements Sections 1–5
CCSS.ELA-Literacy.CCRA.R.4—Interpret words and phrases as they are used in a text, including determining technical, connotative, and figurative meanings, and analyze how specific word choices shape meaning or tone.	Vocabulary Sections 1–5
CCSS.ELA-Literacy.CCRA.R.5—Analyze the structure of texts, including how specific sentences, paragraphs, and larger portions of the text (e.g., a section, chapter, scene, or stanza) relate to each other and the whole.	Analyzing the Literature Sections 1–5; Creating with the Story Elements Sections 1–5
CCSS.ELA-Literacy.CCRA.R.6—Assess how point of view or purpose shapes the content and style of a text.	Making Connections Section 5; Post-Reading Theme Thoughts
CCSS.ELA-Literacy.CCRA.R.10—Read and comprehend complex literary and informational texts independently and proficiently.	Entire Unit
CCSS.ELA-Literacy.CCRA.W.1—Write arguments to support claims in an analysis of substantive topics or texts using valid reasoning and relevant and sufficient evidence.	Reader Response Sections 1, 4–5; Culminating Activity; Post-Reading Response to Literature
CCSS.ELA-Literacy.CCRA.W.2—Write informative/explanatory texts to examine and convey complex ideas and information clearly and accurately through the effective selection, organization, and analysis of content.	Reader Response Sections 1–3; Culminating Activity; Post-Reading Response to Literature
CCSS.ELA-Literacy.CCRA.W.3—Write narratives to develop real or imagined experiences or events using effective technique, well-chosen details and well-structured event sequences.	Reader Response Sections 2–5; Culminating Activity; Post-Reading Response to Literature
CCSS.ELA-Literacy.CCRA.W.4—Produce clear and coherent writing in which the development, organization, and style are appropriate to task, purpose, and audience.	Reader Response Sections 1–5; Creating with the Story Elements Section 2; Culminating Activity; Post-Reading Response to Literature

Correlation to the Standards (cont.)

Standards Correlation Chart (cont.)

Common Core College and Career Readiness Anchor Standard	Section
CCSS.ELA-Literacy.CCRA.W.6—Use technology, including the Internet, to produce and publish writing and to interact and collaborate with others.	Making Connections Sections 1–2, 4; Creating with the Story Elements Sections 3–4; Post-Reading Response to Literature
CCSS.ELA-Literacy.CCRA.W.7—Conduct short as well as more sustained research projects based on focused questions, demonstrating understanding of the subject under investigation.	Making Connections Sections 1–2, 4; Creating with the Story Elements Sections 3–4; Post-Reading Response to Literature
CCSS.ELA-Literacy.CCRA.W.9—Draw evidence from literary or informational texts to support analysis, reflection, and research.	Reader Response Sections 1–5; Post-Reading Response to Literature
CCSS.ELA-Literacy.CCRA.L.1—Demonstrate command of the conventions of standard English grammar and usage when writing or speaking.	Reader Response Sections 1–5; Creating with the Story Elements Section 2; Culminating Activity; Post-Reading Response to Literature
CCSS.ELA-Literacy.CCRA.L.2—Demonstrate command of the conventions of standard English capitalization, punctuation, and spelling when writing.	Reader Response Sections 1–5; Creating with the Story Elements Section 2; Culminating Activity; Post-Reading Response to Literature
CCSS.ELA-Literacy.CCRA.L.4—Determine or clarify the meaning of unknown and multiple-meaning words and phrases by using context clues, analyzing meaningful word parts, and consulting general and specialized reference materials, as appropriate.	Vocabulary Sections 1–5
CCSS.ELA-Literacy.CCRA.L.5—Demonstrate understanding of figurative language, word relationships, and nuances in word meanings.	Vocabulary Sections 1–5; Creating with the Story Elements Section 3
CCSS.ELA-Literacy.CCRA.L.6—Acquire and use accurately a range of general academic and domain-specific words and phrases sufficient for reading, writing, speaking, and listening at the college and career readiness level; demonstrate independence in gathering vocabulary knowledge when encountering an unknown term important to comprehension or expression.	Vocabulary Sections 1–5

TESOL and WIDA Standards

The lessons in this book promote English language development for English language learners. The following TESOL and WIDA English Language Development Standards are addressed through the activities in this book:

- **Standard 1:** English language learners communicate for social and instructional purposes within the school setting.

- **Standard 2:** English language learners communicate information, ideas and concepts necessary for academic success in the content area of language arts.

About the Author—Virginia Hamilton

Born on March 12, 1934, Virginia Esther Hamilton grew up in a large family in Yellow Springs, Ohio. Her family lived on farmland that had belonged to Hamilton's mother's family since Hamilton's grandfather, Levi Perry, was brought to Ohio as an infant by way of the Underground Railway in the late 1850s. From the time she was young, Hamilton devoted herself to writing. She attended Antioch College on a full scholarship, later transferring to Ohio State University.

After college, Hamilton moved to New York City, where she held down several jobs while studying writing and pursuing her dream of becoming a published author. During this time, Hamilton met and married poet Arnold Adoff. After their marriage, Hamilton was able to become a full-time writer, then she continued to write while raising the couple's two children. The family moved to the family farm in Ohio in 1969.

A prolific writer, Hamilton wrote and published 41 books in a variety of genres. Beginning with the 1967 publication of her debut novel, *Zeely*, Hamilton garnered many awards for her outstanding writing and storytelling. She was dubbed the "most honored author in children's literature." *M.C. Higgins, the Great*, published in 1974, is her most honored novel. In the introduction to a later edition, Hamilton describes how M.C. was fully born out of her imagination and that she came to know him as she followed him through the story. *M.C. Higgins, the Great* was the first book to win the Newbery Medal, National Book Award, and *Boston Globe-Horn* Book Award. It also marked the first time an African-American writer was honored with the Newbery Medal.

Hamilton worked as a writer and a lecturer for many years, while living with Adoff in their "dream home" on the farm in Ohio. Their son, Jaime Adoff, is a writer, and their daughter, Leigh Hamilton, is a professional singer. Hamilton died in February 2002.

Possible Texts for Text Comparisons

Hamilton's first book, *Zeely*, tells the story of city girl Geeder, who is sent to spend the summer on her uncle's farm. The visit becomes more fascinating for imaginative Geeder when she meets a strikingly regal local woman and decides she is a Watusi queen. In *Bluish*, 10-year-old Dreenie starts the year at a new school and hesitantly befriends a girl dubbed "Bluish" because of the tint of her skin caused by chemotherapy. Giving voice to another unusual character in *The Planet of Junior Brown*, Hamilton tackles the story of a talented musician trying to survive middle school—and his weight of 300 pounds.

Book Summary of *M.C. Higgins, the Great*

From atop a steel pole, carefully modified with a bicycle seat, 13-year-old Mayo Cornelius, dubbed M.C., can survey his world, keep watch over his younger siblings, and, in his words, "bounce the sun beside me if I want." His family lives in a small home nestled on the slope of a mountain near the Ohio River. M.C.'s mother cleans houses in town, and his father picks up day work at a nearby steel mill. M.C. loves the freedom of his life, but worries about his family's future, concerned that the debris that strip mining companies have deposited on the mountain above the family home poses a threat to their safety.

M.C. hopes that a rumored visit from a man recording talented singers will save the family by bringing his gifted mother a recording contract, fame, and financial security. The man, James Lewis, arrives and records M.C.'s mother, but it becomes clear that she will not be leaving their simple home. During Lewis's visit, M.C. also realizes that his father has refused to face reality, and has no plans to save the home from the threatening slag heap.

M.C. forms a tentative friendship with Lurhetta, the young girl who drove Lewis to town. This relationship makes him newly consider some of the positive and negative aspects of his isolated life in the mountains. Spending time with Lurhetta and his friend Ben, M.C. also realizes that his father's superstitious fear of the "witchy" people who live nearby may be unwarranted.

M.C. decides that he must make a stand against his father's prejudices and intractability. Yet, M.C. is not willing to leave his family and their beloved hillside home. When he starts a project that he hopes will keep his home safe, his father respects his maturity and joins in the effort.

Cross-Curricular Connection

This book is appropriate for social studies and literature studies.

Possible Texts for Text Sets

- Armstrong, William H. *Sounder*. HarperCollins, 2002.
- Curtis, Christopher Paul. *Bud, Not Buddy*. Laurel Leaf, 2004.
- Taylor, Mildred D. *Roll of Thunder, Hear My Cry*. Puffin, 1991.

Name _____

Date _____

Pre-Reading Theme Thoughts

Directions: Read each of the statements in the first column. Decide if you agree or disagree with the statements. Record your opinion by marking an X in Agree or Disagree for each statement. Explain your choices in the fourth column. There are no right or wrong answers.

Statement	Agree	Disagree	Explain Your Answer
You should always be suspicious of strangers.			
Kids should only be friends with people of whom their parents approve.			
You shouldn't dream too big and risk disappointment.			
Older kids should take responsibility for younger kids in the family.			

Vocabulary Overview

Ten key words from this section are provided below with definitions and sentences about how the words are used in the book. Choose one of the vocabulary activity sheets (pages 15 or 16) for students to complete as they read this section. Monitor students as they work to ensure the definitions they have found are accurate and relate to the text. Finally, discuss these important vocabulary words with students. If you think these words or other words in the section warrant more time devoted to them, there are suggestions in the introduction for other vocabulary activities (page 5).

Word	Definition	Sentence about Text
furtively (ch. 1)	done sneakily, to avoid being noticed	M.C. looks around **furtively**, not wanting to be seen greeting the sunrise.
lithe (ch. 1)	limber and graceful	His movements are smooth and **lithe**, almost like a cat's.
ponderous (ch. 1)	slow and awkward	Each swing of the old vine is slow and **ponderous**.
clambering (ch. 1)	climbing with effort or difficulty	M.C. smiles while **clambering** over the lip of the gully, instead of taking the easier path.
premonition (ch. 2)	a strong feeling that something is about to happen	M.C.'s hands start to itch when he has a **premonition** about having a visitor soon.
desolate (ch. 2)	deserted; bleak	Nothing moves in the hot, **desolate** landscape.
seepage (ch. 2)	liquid that passes slowly through small openings	The slimy **seepage** from the spoil heap is allowing the pile to slide down the mountain.
cadence (ch. 3)	the rhythm of a person's voice	M.C.'s yodel has a lilting, rolling **cadence**.
sheepish (ch. 3)	showing embarrassment	M.C.'s father looks **sheepish** when he can't climb very far up the pole.
windfall (ch. 3)	unexpected good fortune	M.C. wins a dollar from his father and is pleased at the unexpected **windfall** of money.

Name _____

Date _____

Understanding Vocabulary Words

Directions: The following words appear in this section of the book. Use context clues and reference materials to determine an accurate definition for each word.

Word	Definition
furtively (ch. 1)	
lithe (ch. 1)	
ponderous (ch. 1)	
clambering (ch. 1)	
premonition (ch. 2)	
desolate (ch. 2)	
seepage (ch. 2)	
cadence (ch. 3)	
sheepish (ch. 3)	
windfall (ch. 3)	

Name _____

Date _____

During-Reading Vocabulary Activity

Directions: As you read these chapters, record at least eight important words on the lines below. Try to find interesting, difficult, intriguing, special, or funny words. Your words can be long or short. They can be hard or easy to spell. After each word, use context clues in the text and reference materials to define the word.

- _____
- _____
- _____
- _____
- _____
- _____
- _____
- _____
- _____
- _____

Directions: Respond to these questions about the words in this section.

1. In chapter 1, the girl moves **warily** along the path. How would one move if feeling wary?

   _____

   _____

2. In chapter 3, M.C. adds things to the pole so that the kids will **cherish** it. What does **cherish** mean and why does M.C. want them to feel that way?

   _____

   _____

Analyzing the Literature

Provided below are discussion questions you can use in small groups, with the whole class, or for written assignments. Each question is given at two levels so you can choose the right question for each group of students. Activity sheets with these questions are provided (pages 18–19) if you want students to write their responses. For each question, a few key discussion points are provided for your reference.

Story Element	■ Level 1	▲ Level 2	Key Discussion Points
Character	Why does M.C. keep his friendship with Ben Killburn a secret?	What does M.C.'s secret friendship with Ben tell you about his father? Do you think the attitudes about the Killburns are fair? Why or why not?	The Killburns are called "witchy" people and locals are suspicious of them. Jones believes the legends and would not want his son playing with a Killburn, so the boys keep their friendship secret. Discuss how people can fear those who have different customs or who look different.
Setting	Describe Sarah's Mountain and the area near it.	How does M.C. feel about Sarah's Mountain? Why is it special to him?	The mountain sits in a lovely, green, undeveloped area near the Ohio River. Recently, a mining company stripped the summit of the mountain. Other nearby hills also have coal seams cut across them. Sarah's Mountain is named for M.C.'s great-grandmother. His family has lived there for generations.
Plot	Why is Mr. Lewis important to M.C.?	Describe M.C.'s mixed emotions about Mr. Lewis and his purpose in coming to see M.C.'s mother.	Lewis will record M.C.'s mother singing. M.C. hopes this will entice his family to move away before the spoil slides. But M.C. also fears the outside world. He worries about his mother leaving, and about how the family would survive a big change.
Character	What goes wrong when Jones and M.C. are playing together in chapter 3?	Explain why Jones says, ". . . because of that pole you think you are some M.C. Higgins, the Great!"	Jones hurts M.C. when he jumps him and squeezes too hard. M.C. is getting to be almost as strong as his father and they are competitive with each other. Jones points out that just because M.C. can swim and climb the pole, he's not that great—his dad taught him. He seems threatened by M.C.

Name _____

Date _____

Analyzing the Literature

Directions: Think about the section you just read. Read each question and state your response with textual evidence.

1. Why does M.C. keep his friendship with Ben Killburn a secret?

   _____

   _____

   _____

   _____

2. Describe Sarah's Mountain and the area near it.

   _____

   _____

   _____

   _____

3. Why is Mr. Lewis important to M.C.?

   _____

   _____

   _____

   _____

4. What goes wrong when Jones and M.C. are playing together in chapter 3?

   _____

   _____

   _____

   _____

▲ Analyzing the Literature

Directions: Think about the section you just read. Read each question and state your response with textual evidence.

1. What does M.C.'s secret friendship with Ben tell you about his father? Do you think the attitudes about the Killburns are fair? Why or why not?

   _____

   _____

   _____

2. How does M.C. feel about Sarah's Mountain? Why is it special to him?

   _____

   _____

   _____

3. Describe M.C.'s mixed emotions about Mr. Lewis and his purpose in coming to see M.C.'s mother.

   _____

   _____

   _____

4. Explain why Jones says, ". . . because of that pole you think you are some M.C. Higgins, the Great!"

   _____

   _____

   _____

Name _____

Date _____

Reader Response

Directions: Choose one of the following prompts about this section to answer. Be sure you include a topic sentence in your response, use textual evidence to support your opinion, and provide a strong conclusion that summarizes your opinion.

Writing Prompts

- **Opinion/Argument Piece**—Which setting would you prefer to live in—where M.C. lives or where you currently live? Explain why your choice is the better place to live. Be persuasive.
- **Informative/Explanatory Piece**—M.C.'s pole plays an important role in his life. Give at least three examples to describe how the pole has helped shape the story so far.

_____

_____

_____

_____

_____

_____

_____

_____

_____

_____

_____

_____

_____

_____

Name _____

Date _____

Close Reading the Literature

Directions: Closely reread the first eight paragraphs of chapter 2, ending with, "'I'm all alone,' M.C. thought." Read each question and then revisit the text to find evidence that supports your answer.

1. According to the text, what is M.C. doing with his feet while swinging on the pole? Why does he eventually stop?

   _____

   _____

   _____

2. What can M.C. see from atop the pole?

   _____

   _____

   _____

3. Describe how high the pole is. Describe where it is placed. Based on the text, what impact does its placement have?

   _____

   _____

   _____

4. What observation does M.C. make about the people he can see walking the hill paths?

   _____

   _____

   _____

Name _____

Date _____

Making Connections–
The Geography of M.C.'s Mountain

Directions: In this section, the author vividly describes Sarah's Mountain and the surrounding area. Create a topographical map of the place where M.C. lives, including labels for the following structures and natural features. If necessary, research what each geographical feature is.

- brier
- coal seam
- foothills
- gully
- ledge

- Ohio River
- outcropping
- pole
- ravine
- spoil heap

- summit
- undergrowth
- vine bridge

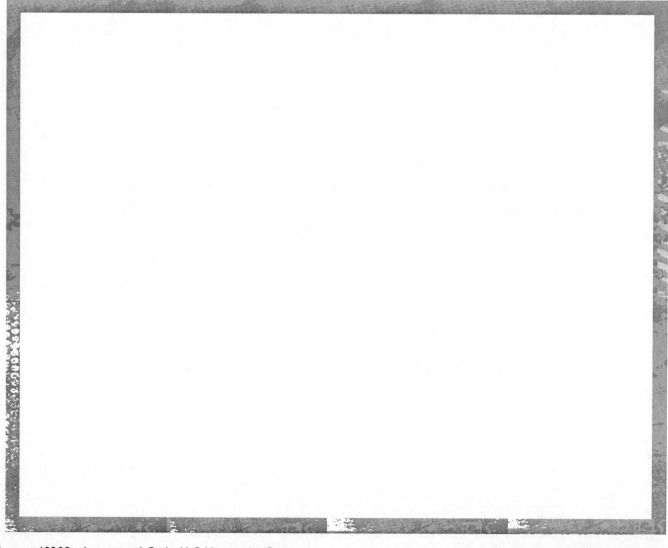

Name _____

Date _____

Creating with the Story Elements

Directions: Thinking about the story elements of character, setting, and plot in a novel is very important to understanding what is happening and why. Complete **one** of the following activities based on what you've read so far. Be creative and have fun!

Characters

Create a Venn diagram that compares M.C. and his father. Think about how they behave with each other in chapter 3. Include at least three differences and three similarities in your diagram.

Setting

Imagine having a pole to sit on in your backyard or on the building where you live. What could you see looking out over your neighborhood? Draw a picture. Label what you can see.

Plot

A cliffhanger is a point in a story where you're not sure what is going to happen next. What is the cliffhanger in this novel so far? Draw a cliff (or an outcropping as described in the book). Label the drawing with the event that sets up the cliffhanger. Then, write three or more ways that the story could progress from there.

Vocabulary Overview

Ten key words from this section are provided below with definitions and sentences about how the words are used in the book. Choose one of the vocabulary activity sheets (pages 25 or 26) for students to complete as they read this section. Monitor students as they work to ensure the definitions they have found are accurate and relate to the text. Finally, discuss these important vocabulary words with students. If you think these words or other words in the section warrant more time devoted to them, there are suggestions in the introduction for other vocabulary activities (page 5).

Word	Definition	Sentence about Text
second sight (ch. 4)	the ability to see into the future	M.C. is so skilled at making out what is around him, Jones sometimes believes his son has **second sight**.
gossamer (ch. 4)	very light and delicate	The sky is dark, without even a streak of purple **gossamer** left in view.
utterly (ch. 5)	completely; absolutely	He stops and stands **utterly** still, trying to think.
smoldering (ch. 5)	burning slowly, with no flame	M.C. uses his handmade torch until it burns out, then throws the **smoldering** mop to the ground.
resignedly (ch. 5)	showing acceptance	M.C. realizes he has been lured to the gully and **resignedly** waits to see what will happen.
revelation (ch. 6)	a surprising fact	Mr. Lewis says it is a **revelation** to him how people have accepted the strip mining without fighting back.
remnant (ch. 6)	a small, leftover piece	Banina has a beautiful **remnant** of carpet from an embassy where she once worked.
impenetrable (ch. 6)	closed off	Jones closes his eyes, looking contented but **impenetrable**.
dread (ch. 6)	great fear and worry	Jones ignores the warnings about the spoil heap, filling M.C. with an uncontrollable feeling of **dread**.
incredulously (ch. 6)	disbelievingly	After hearing Jones's unrealistic plans for dealing with the spoil heap, Mr. Lewis looks at his host **incredulously**.

Name _____

Date _____

Understanding Vocabulary Words

Directions: The following words appear in this section of the book. Use context clues and reference materials to determine an accurate definition for each word.

Word	Definition
second sight (ch. 4)	
gossamer (ch. 4)	
utterly (ch. 5)	
smoldering (ch. 5)	
resignedly (ch. 5)	
revelation (ch. 6)	
remnant (ch. 6)	
impenetrable (ch. 6)	
dread (ch. 6)	
incredulously (ch. 6)	

Name _____

Date _____

During-Reading Vocabulary Activity

Directions: As you read these chapters, record at least eight important words on the lines below. Try to find interesting, difficult, intriguing, special, or funny words. Your words can be long or short. They can be hard or easy to spell. After each word, use context clues in the text and reference materials to define the word.

- _____
- _____
- _____
- _____
- _____
- _____
- _____
- _____

Directions: Respond to these questions about the words in this section.

1. Describe what it would be like to be outside in M.C.'s environment and to hear something **eerie**.

   _____

   _____

2. In chapter 5, M.C. stares straight into the girl's **stricken** eyes. What leads up to that description of her eyes? What happens next to intensify her feelings?

   _____

   _____

Analyzing the Literature

Provided below are discussion questions you can use in small groups, with the whole class, or for written assignments. Each question is given at two levels so you can choose the right question for each group of students. Activity sheets with these questions are provided (pages 28–29) if you want students to write their responses. For each question, a few key discussion points are provided for your reference.

Story Element	■ Level 1	▲ Level 2	Key Discussion Points
Setting	Why does the rainstorm in chapter 4 make M.C. anxious?	The rain in chapter 4 upsets M.C. but not his father. Why do they have different reactions?	M.C. fears that the rain will lubricate the spoil heap and make it slide down the mountain. The mound of debris is a constant source of anxiety for him. Jones disregards M.C.'s concerns and becomes angry when he mentions them. In contrast to his son, he refuses to recognize the threat at all.
Plot	At the end of chapter 4, M.C. describes the events of one of his birthdays. How does the family celebrate?	How does M.C.'s birthday celebration compare to your birthday? How does the day make M.C. feel?	The family waits for M.C.'s mother, Banina, to walk home from work. When she arrives, she brings cake and a practical gift for M.C. The younger kids get small sacks of candy. The family is delighted to be reunited and to have simple pleasures to share. M.C. is "too happy even to say a word of thanks."
Character	What does Banina tell M.C. about the pole and the reason why it stands amid junk in the yard?	Banina tells M.C. why his father put a pole in the yard. What realization does that lead M.C. to have about his father?	The pole is a marker for the dead. Once the yard was full of gravestones, but Banina had Jones remove them. Jones then filled the yard with junk and the pole as a monument. M.C. realizes that Jones's attachment to his ancestors keeps him tied to the mountain. To make Jones leave, he will have to "wrench him from the past."
Plot	What happens when Mr. Lewis returns?	Do you think Mr. Lewis is going to make Banina famous? Why or why not?	Mr. Lewis and the family listen as Banina sings, and Lewis is enthusiastic about her voice. M.C. notices that Lewis makes no mention of taking Banina to Nashville to record music. Instead, the visitor seems more interested in discussing the dangers of the spoil heap. This does not bode well for M.C.'s dreams of using his mother's voice as a way to escape the mountain.

Name _____

Date _____

Analyzing the Literature

Directions: Think about the section you just read. Read each question and state your response with textual evidence.

1. Why does the rainstorm in chapter 4 make M.C. anxious?

   _____

   _____

   _____

   _____

2. At the end of chapter 4, M.C. describes the events of one of his birthdays. How does the family celebrate?

   _____

   _____

   _____

   _____

3. What does Banina tell M.C. about the pole and the reason why it stands amid junk in the yard?

   _____

   _____

   _____

   _____

4. What happens when Mr. Lewis returns?

   _____

   _____

   _____

Name _____

Date _____

▲ Analyzing the Literature

Directions: Think about the section you just read. Read each question and state your response with textual evidence.

1. The rain in chapter 4 upsets M.C. but not his father. Why do they have different reactions?

   _____

   _____

   _____

   _____

2. How does M.C.'s birthday celebration compare to your birthday? How does the day make M.C. feel?

   _____

   _____

   _____

   _____

3. Banina tells M.C. why his father put a pole in the yard. What realization does that lead M.C. to have about his father?

   _____

   _____

   _____

   _____

4. Do you think Mr. Lewis is going to make Banina famous? Why or why not?

   _____

   _____

   _____

Name _____

Date _____

Reader Response

Directions: Choose one of the following prompts about this section to answer. Be sure you include a topic sentence in your response, use textual evidence to support your opinion, and provide a strong conclusion that summarizes your opinion.

Writing Prompts

- **Informative/Explanatory Piece**—Explain how M.C. and his life are similar to or different from yours. Think about the setting where he lives, his responsibilities, and his family. Draw examples for your piece that illustrate details from both his life and yours.
- **Narrative Piece**—Discuss what you think Mr. Lewis will do next. Think about how the visit ended. Balance that against Mama's beautiful singing. Use examples from the story to support your writing.

_____

_____

_____

_____

_____

_____

_____

_____

_____

_____

_____

Name _____

Date _____

Close Reading the Literature

Directions: Closely reread the first eight paragraphs of chapter 5. Read each question and then revisit the text to find evidence that supports your answer.

1. What is M.C. thinking about when the chapter opens? Find two examples in the text that show he is feeling wistful.

   _____

   _____

   _____

   _____

2. What time of day is it? Support your answer with references from the text.

   _____

   _____

   _____

   _____

3. Something catches M.C.'s attention. What words are used in the text to describe what he tries to see?

   _____

   _____

   _____

4. Why is M.C. so intrigued by something he can't identify? Base your answer on this passage and also what you already know about M.C.

   _____

   _____

   _____

Name _____

Date _____

Making Connections—
Creating a New Oral Tradition

In chapter 6, Banina sings songs that have been handed down through the family for many years. The practice of passing down cultural ideas through speech or song, rather than by writing things down, is called the oral tradition.

Directions: Consider the history of your family. What traditions are important in your home or in your culture? Speak with older relatives and ask them to describe events or customs that they would want memorialized for future generations. Write a song that could be passed down as oral tradition in your family.

_____

_____

_____

_____

_____

_____

_____

_____

_____

_____

_____

_____

_____

Name _____

Date _____

Creating with the Story Elements

Directions: Thinking about the story elements of character, setting, and plot in a novel is very important to understanding what is happening and why. Complete **one** of the following activities based on what you've read so far. Be creative and have fun!

Characters

Think of someone that you think M.C. should meet. It must be a real person. It could be someone who could be a role model, someone who could teach him something useful, or someone that could help him. Identify the person and explain why you want to make the introduction.

Setting

Write a persuasive letter from M.C. to his father. It should outline all the reasons Jones needs to think about the threat of the spoil. Make sure that it is logical, well organized, and thoughtful. Be convincing regarding the impact if the spoil slides.

Plot

If a detective suddenly showed up in the story, what might he or she be investigating? Think about the characters, events, and setting. What might the detective discover that could be useful to M.C.?

Understanding Vocabulary Words

Directions: The following words appear in this section of the book. Use context clues and reference materials to determine an accurate definition for each word.

Word	Definition
ginseng (ch. 7)	
brazenly (ch. 7)	
smirked (ch. 8)	
peeved (ch. 8)	
offense (ch. 8)	
skittish (ch. 8)	
futilely (ch. 9)	
dislodge (ch. 9)	
jostling (ch. 9)	
bedraggled (ch. 9)	

Analyzing the Literature

Provided below are discussion questions you can use in small groups, with the whole class, or for written assignments. Each question is given at two levels so you can choose the right question for each group of students. Activity sheets with these questions are provided (pages 38–39) if you want students to write their responses. For each question, a few key discussion points are provided for your reference.

Story Element	■ Level 1	▲ Level 2	Key Discussion Points
Character	At the beginning of chapter 7, why does Banina wake up M.C. very early in the morning?	Why do you think Banina insists that M.C. get up early to go swimming with her, without the other kids?	Banina wakes up M.C. to swim with her before she leaves for work. She has little leisure time, so she has to start her day very early. Banina may insist that M.C. go with her so that she can have private time with her oldest child. She gives M.C. advice and tells him stories during their time together.
Plot	What happens with M.C. and the girl in the water tunnel? How does she mislead M.C.?	M.C. feels several emotions after he and the girl make it through the water tunnel. What are they?	The girl convinces M.C. to take her through the water tunnel. She never mentions that she can't swim, and both of them almost drown. M.C. is angry at her for not telling him that she can't swim. He's upset with himself for not asking. He's proud that he got her through anyway, and he's shaken by how dangerous it was.
Setting	Who knows more about the world, the girl or M.C.? Why is this?	The girl tells M.C. about all the places she has seen. Why does she have such independence? Is this freedom an advantage or disadvantage over M.C.'s lifestyle?	The girl is more worldly than M.C. She has her own car and has traveled extensively, while M.C. has never left the hills around his home. The girl has no family except a mother who seems happy to let her daughter go her own way. The girl's freedom to travel is enviable. However, she does not have a loving family or a stable home.
Plot	At the end of chapter 9, Jones teases M.C. about having a crush on the girl. Do you think he does? Why or why not?	Why does Jones tell M.C. that he'll be nice to the girl? What does this tell you about their relationship?	M.C. probably has a crush on the girl. He impulsively kisses her, he worries about her and brings her home, and he seems fascinated by everything about her. Jones knows that she is important to M.C., even if M.C. won't admit it. Despite their rivalry, Jones obviously wants M.C. to be happy. He promises to be polite so M.C. won't be embarrassed in front of his guest.

Name _____

Date _____

■ Analyzing the Literature

Directions: Think about the section you just read. Read each question and state your response with textual evidence.

1. At the beginning of chapter 7, why does Banina wake up M.C. very early in the morning?

   _____

   _____

   _____

   _____

2. What happens with M.C. and the girl in the water tunnel? How does she mislead M.C.?

   _____

   _____

   _____

   _____

3. Who knows more about the world, the girl or M.C.? Why is this?

   _____

   _____

   _____

   _____

4. At the end of chapter 9, Jones teases M.C. about having a crush on the girl. Do you think he does? Why or why not?

   _____

   _____

   _____

▲ Analyzing the Literature

Directions: Think about the section you just read. Read each question and state your response with textual evidence.

1. Why do you think Banina insists that M.C. get up early to go swimming with her, without the other kids?

   _____

   _____

   _____

   _____

2. M.C. feels several emotions after he and the girl make it through the water tunnel. What are they?

   _____

   _____

   _____

   _____

3. The girl tells M.C. about all the places she has seen. Why does she have such independence? Is this freedom an advantage or disadvantage over M.C.'s lifestyle?

   _____

   _____

   _____

4. Why does Jones tell M.C. that he'll be nice to the girl? What does this tell you about their relationship?

   _____

   _____

   _____

Name _____

Date _____

Reader Response

Directions: Choose one of the following prompts about this section to answer. Be sure you include a topic sentence in your response, use textual evidence to support your opinion, and provide a strong conclusion that summarizes your opinion.

Writing Prompts

- **Informative/Explanatory Piece**—Banina tells M.C. a story about the "witchy" powers of the Killburn family. Should this story be taken at face value? What non-mystical explanations might there be for the actions of Viola Killburn and the effect they had on the injured boy?
- **Narrative Piece**—Assume the role of an advice columnist. Write a letter to M.C. that gives him advice about the girl. Explain whether having a crush on her is a good idea. If so, describe how he can win her affection. If the crush is not a good idea, describe how he should handle it—and his heartbreak.

_____

_____

_____

_____

_____

_____

_____

_____

_____

_____

_____

_____

_____

Close Reading the Literature

Directions: Closely reread the first section of chapter 9, ending with, "Be M.C. Higgins, the Great." Read each question and then revisit the text to find evidence that supports your answer.

1. How is the feeling of being in deep water described in the first paragraph? Include M.C.'s reaction to it.

    _____

    _____

    _____

    _____

2. How does the girl's pressure affect M.C. as he swims midway through the tunnel? Use text evidence to explain your answer.

    _____

    _____

    _____

3. M.C. thinks this, "Won't make it." What is the question he desperately wishes he had asked the girl?

    _____

    _____

    _____

4. Use text evidence to describe how M.C. feels just before he gets his second wind.

    _____

    _____

    _____

Chapters 7–9

Name _____
Date _____

Making Connections—Making the Goal

Directions: Writers often create goals for their characters. In chapters 8 and 9, the girl has a clear goal: swimming through the water tunnel. Complete this goal chart, showing her reasons, facts about the challenge, and possible outcomes.

Goal: Swimming through the water tunnel

↓

Reason:

Reason:

↓

Fact:

Fact:

Fact:

↓

Outcome:

Outcome:

42   #40209—Instructional Guide: M.C. Higgins, the Great   © Shell Education

Name

Date

Creating with the Story Elements

Directions: Thinking about the story elements of character, setting, and plot in a novel is very important to understanding what is happening and why. Complete **one** of the following activities based on what you've read so far. Be creative and have fun!

Characters

Create a word splash that describes M.C. Higgins' character. Draw an image of a drop of water in the center of a piece of paper. Choose ten to fifteen words that describe M.C., based on this section of the novel. "Splash" drawings of drops of water on a piece of paper. Write each of your words in the drops.

Setting

Make a drawing of the underwater tunnel based on the descriptions in chapters 8 and 9. Make it a cutaway, showing the swimmers going through the tunnel, the fish, the colors caused by the sun, and so forth.

Plot

In chapter 9, M.C. realizes that the girl isn't well prepared for camping. Make a list of recommendations for someone who is going to be camping for several days. Use advice inspired by the chapter and from other sources, such as your experience, the Internet, and library research.

Vocabulary Overview

Ten key words from this section are provided below with definitions and sentences about how the words are used in the book. Choose one of the vocabulary activity sheets (pages 45 or 46) for students to complete as they read this section. Monitor students as they work to ensure the definitions they have found are accurate and relate to the text. Finally, discuss these important vocabulary words with students. If you think these words or other words in the section warrant more time devoted to them, there are suggestions in the introduction for other vocabulary activities (page 5).

Word	Definition	Sentence about Text
outlandish (ch. 10)	unusual or bizarre	The conversation stops when they hear **outlandish** yelling from outside.
indignantly (ch. 10)	angrily; showing displeasure at something unfair	Lurhetta looks at Jones **indignantly**, surprised at his rudeness.
frantically (ch. 11)	wildly and desperately	The rabbit races **frantically** in the trap, but can't escape.
patina (ch. 11)	a sheen or film on the surface of something	Years of wind, rain, and sun have worn down the path and given it a distinctive **patina**.
compound (ch. 11)	collection of buildings	There are sheds, barns, and farmhouses on the Mound, the Killburn **compound**.
amiable (ch. 12)	pleasant; friendly	The many family members at the Mound interact in a relaxed, **amiable** way.
precariously (ch. 12)	uncertainly	M.C. perches **precariously** on the hub, not wanting to ask for help.
inflection (ch. 12)	modulation of the voice	Mrs. Killburn's speaks with a rising **inflection** that is typical of hill women.
prosperous (ch. 12)	well-off financially	Mr. Killburn's beautifully stitched overalls make him look like the perfect example of the **prosperous** farmer.
quavered (ch. 12)	shook	M.C. is so mad at Ben that when he speaks his voice **quavers**.

Name _____

Date _____

Understanding Vocabulary Words

Directions: The following words appear in this section of the book. Use context clues and reference materials to determine an accurate definition for each word.

Word	Definition
outlandish (ch. 10)	
indignantly (ch. 10)	
frantically (ch. 11)	
patina (ch. 11)	
compound (ch. 11)	
amiable (ch. 12)	
precariously (ch. 12)	
inflection (ch. 12)	
prosperous (ch. 12)	
quavered (ch. 12)	

Name _____

Date _____

During-Reading Vocabulary Activity

Directions: As you read these chapters, record at least eight important words on the lines below. Try to find interesting, difficult, intriguing, special, or funny words. Your words can be long or short. They can be hard or easy to spell. After each word, use context clues in the text and reference materials to define the word.

- _____
- _____
- _____
- _____
- _____
- _____
- _____
- _____

Directions: Respond to these questions about these words in this section.

1. M.C. watches Lurhetta with **sullen** eyes while Jones fixes his special soup. What does **sullen** mean? Why does M.C. feel sullen?

   _____

   _____

2. Mr. Killburn has a unique take on vegetables. He compares them to human bodies. What three options does he suggest for dealing with a vegetable that gets the **blight**?

   _____

   _____

Analyzing the Literature

Provided below are discussion questions you can use in small groups, with the whole class, or for written assignments. Each question is given at two levels so you can choose the right question for each group of students. Activity sheets with these questions are provided (pages 48–49) if you want students to write their responses. For each question, a few key discussion points are provided for your reference.

Story Element	■ Level 1	▲ Level 2	Key Discussion Points
Character	What is the girl's real name? Why doesn't she tell people her real name often?	How does Jones help Lurhetta feel better about her name?	The girl's name is Lurhetta Outlaw. She doesn't talk about her name because people laugh or think she's lying. She also worries that she may have had criminals as ancestors. Jones tells her not to be ashamed of who she is. He also points out that "outlaw" can have different meanings and might not be a bad thing.
Character	How does Jones treat the icemen?	Why does Jones treat the icemen so rudely? How does Lurhetta respond to witnessing this interaction between hill people?	Jones treats the icemen with contempt, as if they are barely human. Jones's behavior stems from a long-standing local fear of the "witchy" men. They are reviled because they act differently from other hill folk. Lurhetta is shocked by Jones's behavior, pointing out that he treated the men "like dirt."
Plot	What triggers the trip to Ben's house? How does M.C. feel about going there?	How does Lurhetta manipulate things so she can visit Ben's home? Why do you think M.C. decides to go along?	Lurhetta is curious to see Ben's home. She claims that she is thirsty, but doesn't want to drink from the stream. M.C. is afraid to go to Ben's, but in the end he comes along. He wants to show Lurhetta that he isn't afraid, and also perhaps show her that he is not as prejudiced as his father.
Setting	Describe the area where Ben lives.	Contrast Lurhetta's reaction to the setting of Ben's home with M.C.'s. Why are they so different?	Ben lives in a large compound of farm buildings called the Mound, connected by a web of vines. Family members of all ages interact pleasantly. The people seem prosperous. Lurhetta loves it and wants to see everything. M.C. is uncomfortable. He believes that these are abnormal, supernatural people.

Name _____

Date _____

◼ Analyzing the Literature

Directions: Think about the section you just read. Read each question and state your response with textual evidence.

1. What is the girl's real name? Why doesn't she tell people her real name often?

_____

_____

_____

_____

2. How does Jones treat the icemen?

_____

_____

_____

_____

3. What triggers the trip to Ben's house? How does M.C. feel about going there?

_____

_____

_____

_____

4. Describe the area where Ben lives.

_____

_____

_____

_____

Name _____

Date _____

▲ Analyzing the Literature

Directions: Think about the section you just read. Read each question and state your response with textual evidence.

1. How does Jones help Lurhetta feel better about her name?

   _____

   _____

   _____

   _____

2. Why does Jones treat the icemen so rudely? How does Lurhetta respond to witnessing this interaction between hill people?

   _____

   _____

   _____

   _____

3. How does Lurhetta manipulate things so she can visit Ben's home? Why do you think M.C. decides to go along?

   _____

   _____

   _____

   _____

4. Contrast Lurhetta's reaction to the setting of Ben's home with M.C.'s. Why are they so different?

   _____

   _____

   _____

Name _____

Date _____

Reader Response

Directions: Choose one of the following prompts about this section to answer. Be sure you include a topic sentence in your response, use textual evidence to support your opinion, and provide a strong conclusion that summarizes your opinion.

Writing Prompts

- **Narrative Piece**—Discuss the problems that Luhretta Outlaw faces because she has such a distinctive name. What would you do in her place? What can you do to help others who might be teased about their names?
- **Opinion/Argument Piece**—M.C. catches and kills rabbits to feed his family. The Killburn children are not allowed to kill animals to eat them. Do you think it's okay to kill animals for meat, or do you agree with the Killburn policy?

_____

_____

_____

_____

_____

_____

_____

_____

_____

_____

_____

_____

_____

_____

_____

Name _____

Date _____

Close Reading the Literature

Directions: Closely reread the section near the beginning of chapter 12 that begins, "The effect from guidelines to hub . . . ." End with, "M.C. watched her, feeling a growing jealousy, he didn't know why." Read each question and then revisit the text to find evidence that supports your answer.

1. How does the text describe the way the children look, together on the hub?

   _____

   _____

   _____

   _____

2. What specific jobs do the older children perform, using the weave as transportation?

   _____

   _____

   _____

3. A *simile* is a description that compares two things, using the word *like*. What simile in the text describes the babies who are too small for the hub?

   _____

   _____

   _____

4. How does the text describe Lurhetta's reaction as she observes the idyllic dynamic of the Killburn family?

   _____

   _____

   _____

Name _____

Date _____

Making Connections–Snakes Alive!

Directions: The Killburn family compound is home to many kinds of snakes, which live in harmony with the humans. This seems strange because most people avoid snakes. Many people have misconceptions about this usually harmless reptile. Research snakes on the Internet or in the library. Create a true or false test with facts about snakes. Find a partner and give the test. See if your partner can get a perfect score.

Check Your Snake IQ	True	False
1.		
2.		
3.		
4.		
5.		
6.		
7.		
8.		
9.		
10.		
Score: _____		

Name _____

Date _____

Creating with the Story Elements

Directions: Thinking about the story elements of character, setting, and plot in a novel is very important to understanding what is happening and why. Complete **one** of the following activities based on what you've read so far. Be creative and have fun!

Characters

Which character in the novel do you like the least? Create a two-column chart that lists your dislikes on the left and a reason for each dislike on the right. Consider at least five traits such as behavior, speech, attitude, thoughts, emotions, etc.

Setting

Create a birds-eye view of the web in the Killburn compound. Use a shoebox for a 3-D version or draw a top-down picture. Be sure to connect the buildings, gardens, and people with a web.

Plot

Create a story web that captures the key plot points of the story so far. The plot points do not need to be in chronological order. Do include key events, such as the visit to Ben's compound.

Vocabulary Overview

Ten key words from this section are provided below with definitions and sentences about how the words are used in the book. Choose one of the vocabulary activity sheets (pages 55 or 56) for students to complete as they read this section. Monitor students as they work to ensure the definitions they have found are accurate and relate to the text. Finally, discuss these important vocabulary words with students. If you think these words or other words in the section warrant more time devoted to them, there are suggestions in the introduction for other vocabulary activities (page 5).

Word	Definition	Sentence about Text
rumpled (ch. 13)	disheveled	After his walk up the mountain, Mr. Lewis looks **rumpled** instead of tidy.
despair (ch. 13)	hopelessness	Banina's face betrays a quick moment of **despair** when she admits how tired she is.
frayed (ch. 13)	unraveled at the edges	Jones's shirt is **frayed** from wear, but clean and starched.
perish (ch. 13)	die	M.C. feels his hopes sink and **perish** at the news that Mr. Lewis won't try to sell Banina's voice.
qualm (ch. 13)	an uneasy misgiving	M.C. finds the he can lie about Mr. Lewis without a **qualm**.
predicament (ch. 13)	a difficult situation	Jones assures M.C. that Lurhetta is capable of dealing with any **predicament** she might face.
inkling (ch. 14)	hint	M.C. feels an odd **inkling** of something to come.
rancid (ch. 14)	smelling or tasting unpleasant	M.C. stabs the earth, turning up rocks and dirt that feel cool and smell slightly **rancid**.
revulsion (ch. 14)	disgust	Jones shudders in **revulsion** when he looks at Ben.
solemnly (ch. 14)	earnestly; gravely	Jones **solemnly** asks Ben a question about his friendship with M.C.

Understanding Vocabulary Words

Directions: The following words appear in this section of the book. Use context clues and reference materials to determine an accurate definition for each word.

Word	Definition
rumpled (ch. 13)	
despair (ch. 13)	
frayed (ch. 13)	
perish (ch. 13)	
qualm (ch. 13)	
predicament (ch. 13)	
inkling (ch. 14)	
rancid (ch. 14)	
revulsion (ch. 14)	
solemnly (ch. 14)	

Name _____

Date _____

During-Reading Vocabulary Activity

Directions: As you read these chapters, choose five important words from the story. Use these words to complete the word flow chart below. On each arrow, write a word. In each box, explain how the connected pair of words relates to each other. An example for the words *despair* and *perish* has been done for you.

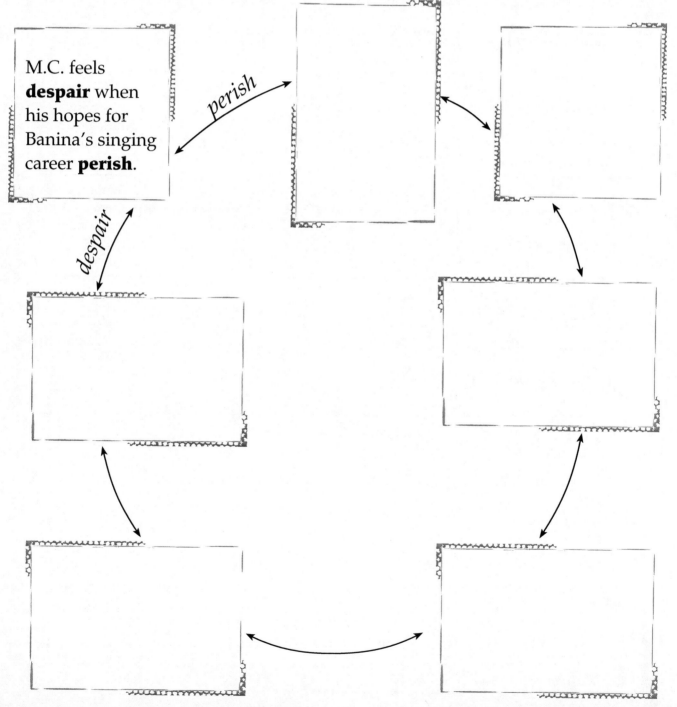

M.C. feels **despair** when his hopes for Banina's singing career **perish**.

perish

despair

Analyzing the Literature

Provided below are discussion questions you can use in small groups, with the whole class, or for written assignments. Each question is given at two levels so you can choose the right question for each group of students. Activity sheets with these questions are provided (pages 58–59) if you want students to write their responses. For each question, a few key discussion points are provided for your reference.

Story Element	■ Level 1	▲ Level 2	Key Discussion Points
Character	What bad news does Mr. Lewis give M.C.?	What is Mr. Lewis's real purpose in recording Mama's voice? Why do you think he bothers to come back to the house?	Mr. Lewis is a folk music collector. He records singers but is not involved with selling music. He wants to record Banina's voice for his collection not for a music contract. He also doesn't think Banina is suited for the stage. Mr. Lewis returns because he does not want to hurt M.C. and he worries about him.
Setting	What does it look like outside when M.C. wakes up at the beginning of chapter 14?	Describe how the fog affects M.C.'s walk through the hills. What mood does the fog help set in the novel?	The mountain is closed in by the thickest fog M.C. has ever seen. He says it looks like he's on the moon. Heading to the lake, M.C. has to touch things to find his way. He feels discombobulated. The mountain pass feels abnormally quiet. There is a mood of apprehension.
Plot	Where is Lurhetta? What does she leave for M.C.?	How does M.C. react to finding out that Lurhetta is gone? Why do you think she leaves the knife behind?	Lurhetta has disappeared. Her tent and other belongings are gone. The only thing she leaves, stuck purposefully into the ground, is her hunting knife. She may have left it as a reminder of how she and M.C. met, as an indication that she could not kill an animal, or because she knew M.C. would recognize it as hers. M.C. is shocked and sad that she is gone.
Plot	Why does M.C. call Ben out from hiding, right in front of Jones?	In what two ways does M.C. assert his independence, in defiance of Jones, in chapter 14?	M.C. tells his father that from now on he will choose his own friends. He calls Ben out into the open to show Jones that he will no longer hew to his father's prejudiced beliefs. M.C. also decides that he can't ignore the threat of the spoil heap. He begins to tear apart the junk pile in the yard, using the materials to build a wall to protect the house.

Name _____

Date _____

■ Analyzing the Literature

Directions: Think about the section you just read. Read each question and state your response with textual evidence.

1. What bad news does Mr. Lewis give M.C.?

   _____

   _____

   _____

   _____

2. What does it look like outside when M.C. wakes up at the beginning of chapter 14?

   _____

   _____

   _____

   _____

3. Where is Lurhetta? What does she leave for M.C.?

   _____

   _____

   _____

   _____

4. Why does M.C. call Ben out from hiding, right in front of Jones?

   _____

   _____

   _____

   _____

Name _____

Date _____

▲ Analyzing the Literature

Directions: Think about the section you just read. Read each question and state your response with textual evidence.

1. What is Mr. Lewis's real purpose in recording Mama's voice? Why do you think he bothers to come back to the house?

   _____

   _____

   _____

   _____

2. Describe how the fog affects M.C.'s walk through the hills. What mood does the fog help set in the novel?

   _____

   _____

   _____

   _____

3. How does M.C. react to finding out that Lurhetta is gone? Why do you think she leaves the knife behind?

   _____

   _____

   _____

4. In what two ways does M.C. assert his independence, in defiance of Jones, in chapter 14?

   _____

   _____

   _____

Name _____

Date _____

Reader Response

Directions: Choose one of the following prompts about this section to answer. Be sure you include a topic sentence in your response, use textual evidence to support your opinion, and provide a strong conclusion that summarizes your opinion.

Writing Prompts

- **Narrative Piece**—It can be hard to admit when you've been wrong. Think about a time in the past when an adult in your life acknowledged a wrongdoing. Compare it to what Jones does at the end of the novel to show that he supports M.C.
- **Opinion/Argument Piece**—Who do you think is more stubborn, M.C. or Jones? Write a convincing argument for your choice, one that gives examples of the stubborn behaviors.

_____
_____
_____
_____
_____
_____
_____
_____
_____
_____
_____
_____
_____
_____

Name _____

Date _____

Close Reading the Literature

Directions: Closely reread the section toward the end of chapter 14 that begins with, "No reply." Read to the end of the chapter. Read each question and then revisit the text to find evidence that supports your answer.

1. What does Jones look like after he comes out from under the porch? Use text evidence in your description.

   _____

   _____

   _____

2. Find two examples in the text that tell you that Jones is carrying something heavy.

   _____

   _____

   _____

3. What reason does M.C. give in the text for why his father gives him the gravestone? Use what you know about Jones and write another reason that is implied by the story.

   _____

   _____

   _____

4. Find the sentence in the book that describes how M.C. feels about his work. Why does he feel this way?

   _____

   _____

   _____

Name _____

Date _____

Making Connections–Is M.C. Really Great?

Directions: The expression, "M.C. Higgins, the Great," is used several times in the novel by M.C. and by other characters. Think about the idea of greatness. What makes a person truly great? Fill in the T-chart below. On one side, list things that M.C. himself might name if **he** were asked to describe why he is great. On the other side, list characteristics or actions of M.C. that **you** think make him great.

What M.C. Considers Great About Himself	What You Consider Great About M.C.

Name _____

Date _____

Creating with the Story Elements

Directions: Thinking about the story elements of character, setting, and plot in a novel is very important to understanding what is happening and why. Complete **one** of the following activities based on what you've read so far. Be creative and have fun!

Characters

What would Lurhetta write on a postcard to M.C.? Would she apologize for leaving? Would she explain why she left the knife? Would she describe where she is now? You decide—and create the postcard, including a picture of where she is now.

Setting

An epitaph is a short statement that is engraved onto a headstone. Research beautifully written epitaphs on the Internet, or visit a cemetery in your community. Create an epitaph for Sarah's gravestone that fits what you know about her.

Plot

The encounters with Mr. Lewis and Lurhetta awaken something new in M.C. Although he still feels strong ties to his home and his family, he also feels a longing to experience things outside of the hills. Can you relate to M.C.'s desire for an identity separate from home and family? Write about something that is important to you—it could be music, an art, a sport, a travel destination, or any interest—that you came to without your family's guidance. How were you influenced to try this, at first? What does it mean to you?

Name _____

Date _____

Post-Reading Theme Thoughts

Directions: Read each of the statements in the first column. Choose a main character from *M.C. Higgins, the Great*. Think about that character's point of view. From that character's perspective, decide if the character would agree or disagree with the statements. Record the character's opinion by marking an X in Agree or Disagree for each statement. Explain your choices in the fourth column using text evidence.

Character I Chose: _____

Statement	Agree	Disagree	Explain Your Answer
You should always be suspicious of strangers.			
Kids should only be friends with people of whom their parents approve.			
You shouldn't dream too big and risk disappointment.			
Older kids should take responsibility for younger kids in the family.			

Name _____

Date _____

Culminating Activity: The World of M.C.

Directions: The setting of *M.C. Higgins, the Great* is an important ingredient in telling M.C.'s story. Analyze the setting of the novel. Get clues about the setting from the text and also from the copyright page—for example, look at when Virginia Hamilton wrote the book. If your copy has the introduction that the author added in 1999, read that as well. Then, complete this summary chart. Some answers may need to be inferences.

1. Where does the story take place?	
2. When does the story take place?	
3. What season is it?	
4. What is the weather like?	
5. What is the geography of the setting?	
6. What industry affects the look of the area?	
7. What challenges does the setting present for outsiders?	
8. What dangers does the setting pose for M.C. and his family?	

Name _____

Date _____

Culminating Activity: M.C., the Movie

Directions: Many great works of literature are eventually adapted and made into movies. Imagine that you are involved in creating a feature film version of *M.C. Higgins, the Great*. Choose one of the following projects to complete.

- You have been asked to create a trailer for the film. Plan the scenes that would be included in the trailer. Choose three or four scenes from the book that encapsulate the "feel" of the novel and the spirit of the main characters. Write a summary of how each scene would be incorporated into the trailer, justifying your scene choices.

- You have written a script for the movie version of the story. However, the director wants an updated story, set in modern times. What would you change to make the story more current? Describe your changes and the implications for the story. For example, how would the story change if the characters had cell phones? Be thorough.

- You have been hired as a location scout, to find an outdoor area for filming the movie. You also have to plan the sets for the movie (the junk pile and the pole in the yard, the water tunnel, the Killburns' compound, etc.) Make a plan for the key scenes, fully describing the features that are necessary for each of the settings.

Name _____

Date _____

Comprehension Assessment

Directions: Circle the best response to each question.

1. What is the meaning of the verb *stalk* as it is used in the book?

    A. follow

    B. hunt

    C. trap

    D. trick

2. Which two details from the book best support your answer to question 1?

    E. "Inside was the rabbit racing frantically . . . ."

    F. "'Wouldn't have hurt you,' he called."

    G. "M.C. always felt bigger and stronger around Ben."

    H. "The thought that Ben was nearby but unseen was all right with M.C."

3. What is the main idea of the text below?

    > "M.C. looked at the knife where blood streaks clung to the steel. He glanced over at Ben, who watched his every move. He took the knife blade between his finger and thumb and called softly to Ben, 'Coming at you.'
    >
    > "Ben had time to duck away as the knife whizzed through the air and hit the post. It struck and trembled on its point a moment before it fell from the wood. Ben scrambled for the knife, found it and headed for the stream to clean it."

    A. M.C. and Ben spend a lot of time at Ben's home.

    B. M.C. is jealous of Ben and wants to hurt him.

    C. Ben and M.C. trust each other, and work well together.

    D. M.C. upsets Lurhetta because he uses her knife.

4. Which detail from the novel best supports your answer to question 3?

    E. "Ben knows what I'm doing almost as soon as I do."

    F. "'You could have hit him!' she said . . . ."

    G. "His voice quavered, as anger at Ben shook him."

    H. "You had to go use my knife—that's awful."

Comprehension Assessment (cont.)

5. Which statement best expresses one of the themes of the book?

    A. Parents know best for their children.

    B. Travel can be exciting and fulfilling.

    C. Strip mining can be good for the economy.

    D. Friendship can rise above fear and prejudice.

6. Which detail from the book provides the best evidence for your answer to number 5?

    E. M.C. makes friends with Lurhetta and Mr. Lewis.

    F. M.C. stands up to his father, saying that Ben is his friend.

    G. M.C. dreams that his mother will become famous.

    H. M.C. plans to get a job working for the Killburns.

7. What is the purpose of this sentence written about Jones in the last chapter? "That look of closed stubbornness seemed to melt from his face as he glanced over where M.C.'s back was bent to his task."

_____

_____

_____

_____

_____

_____

_____

8. What other quotation from the story serves a similar purpose?

    A. "For an instant his eyes were full of pride."

    B. "The children stopped their work to stare."

    C. "He turned and walked through the children . . . ."

    D. "They all went back to work when M.C. started digging a place for the stone."

Response to Literature: Coming of Age

Directions: *M.C. Higgins, the Great* is a type of story known as a coming-of-age tale. This kind of story focuses on the personal growth of a character who is changing from a child into an adult. In this novel, teenage M.C. struggles to reconcile two opposing forces. The first is his love for and loyalty to his family—particularly his father—their traditions and their mountain home. The second is the influence of the outside world—represented by Mr. Lewis and Lurhetta—which helps him see that the things he accepted as a child are not always right. Based on your reading of the novel, which of these forces will "win" as M.C. reaches adulthood? Why? How will his life change because of the personal growth he experiences during the three days described in the novel?

_____

_____

_____

_____

_____

_____

_____

_____

_____

_____

_____

_____

_____

_____

_____

_____

Name _____

Date _____

Response to Literature Rubric

Directions: Use this rubric to evaluate student responses.

	Exceptional Writing	Quality Writing	Developing Writing
Focus and Organization	☐ States a clear opinion and elaborates well. Engages the reader from the opening hook through the middle to the conclusion. Demonstrates clear understanding of the intended audience and purpose of the piece.	☐ Provides a clear and consistent opinion. Maintains a clear perspective and supports it through elaborating details. Makes the opinion clear in the opening hook and summarizes well in the conclusion.	☐ Provides an inconsistent point of view. Does not support the topic adequately or misses pertinent information. Provides lack of clarity in the beginning, middle, and conclusion.
Text Evidence	☐ Provides comprehensive and accurate support. Includes relevant and worthwhile text references.	☐ Provides limited support. Provides few supporting text references.	☐ Provides very limited support for the text. Provides no supporting text references.
Written Expression	☐ Uses descriptive and precise language with clarity and intention. Maintains a consistent voice and uses an appropriate tone that supports meaning. Uses multiple sentence types and transitions well between ideas.	☐ Uses a broad vocabulary. Maintains a consistent voice and supports a tone and feelings through language. Varies sentence length and word choices.	☐ Uses a limited and unvaried vocabulary. Provides an inconsistent or weak voice and tone. Provides little to no variation in sentence type and length.
Language Conventions	☐ Capitalizes, punctuates, and spells accurately. Demonstrates complete thoughts within sentences, with accurate subject-verb agreement. Uses paragraphs appropriately and with clear purpose.	☐ Capitalizes, punctuates, and spells accurately. Demonstrates complete thoughts within sentences and appropriate grammar. Paragraphs are properly divided and supported.	☐ Incorrectly capitalizes, punctuates, and spells. Uses fragmented or run-on sentences. Utilizes poor grammar overall. Paragraphs are poorly divided and developed.

The responses provided here are just examples of what students may answer. Many accurate responses are possible for the questions throughout this unit.

During-Reading Vocabulary Activity—Section 1: Chapters 1–3 (page 16)

1. If feeling **wary**, one would look around nervously, checking behind him or her, perhaps walking slowly.

2. To **cherish** means to hold something dear. M.C. has strong feelings about his pole and he wants his siblings to feel the same way.

Close Reading the Literature—Section 1: Chapters 1–3 (page 21)

1. M.C. is pedaling on the bike pedals he attached to the top of the pole. He stops because he becomes dizzy and worries he might lose his balance.

2. From atop the pole, M.C. can see the Ohio River, the hills, the sky, and people walking the hill paths.

3. The pole is 40 feet high. It is placed on the outcropping near the family home. It is higher that the house and the trees, so it provides a spectacular view.

4. M.C. says that the people think they are absolutely alone, and have no inkling his eyes are upon them.

During-Reading Vocabulary Activity—Section 2: Chapters 4–6 (page 26)

1. **Eerie** means mysterious, strange, and frightening. Because M.C. is outside near the gully, hearing something that has an eerie rhythm could be unnerving or scary.

2. The girls' eyes are **stricken** because M.C. has sneaked up on her in the dark, and the two are engaged in a struggle. They both hold knives. Then M.C. lightly kisses the girl, which increases her terror.

Close Reading the Literature—Section 2: Chapters 4–6 (page 31)

1. As the chapter opens, M.C. is thinking about what it is like when his mother comes home. He sits there for a long time. He notes that he doesn't think he will have any more birthdays at his home.

2. It is evening. The sun has slipped down the side of the mountain and toward the west.

3. M.C. sees something near the river that is described with these words: glinted, flashed, sparkle, glitter.

4. Things usually don't glint that far from the river. The sparkle vanishes at times. M.C. feels confident that he knows everything about his environment. This sight makes him anxious because he can't easily identify what it is.

Close Reading the Literature—Section 3: Chapters 7–9 (page 41)

1. The water is a pressure of "delicious weight." It strips all feeling away, possesses it, and touches along every inch of M.C. He says he likes nothing better than being in the deep.

2. The "dead pressure" of the girl drags M.C. down. His back hits the side of the tunnel.

3. M.C. realizes that he never asked the girl whether she can swim.

4. Before getting his second wind, M.C.'s lungs hurt from lack of air. His chest burns. His legs are still loose and working.

During-Reading Vocabulary Activity—Section 4: Chapters 10–12 (page 46)

1. **Sullen** means bad-tempered and unhappy. M.C. is sullen because he is jealous of the easy rapport between Lurhetta and Jones.

2. If a vegetable gets the **blight**, Mr. Killburn suggests that one can cut away the bad piece, heal the vegetable, or eat it anyway.

Close Reading the Literature—Section 4: Chapters 10–12 (page 51)

1. The children sit together on the net. They have varying colors of red hair. M.C. thinks they look like a "fresh bunch of bright flowers, jumbled and tossed by breezes," their stems dangling down.

2. The older children drop beneath the nets and pull weeds and fill bushel baskets with vegetables.

3. The babies are said to look "like sweet cinnamon lumps."

4. Lurhetta, who has no family of her own, sighs in awe.

Close Reading the Literature—Section 5: Chapters 13–14 (page 61)

1. When Jones comes out from under the porch he is covered with dust—it is in his hair, on his trousers, and on his face.

2. Jones strains under the weight of the thing he is carrying, and he lurches as he walks.

3. M.C. says that Jones got the gravestone because it will help make the wall strong. Another reason could be that Jones is symbolically supporting M.C. Handing over Sarah's gravestone, a symbol of the past that holds Jones so strongly, is a tacit way of showing that he accepts that things must change in the future.

4. M.C. knows that his "work is urgent." He feels that way because he senses that clouds are massing and a storm is coming. The rain is slowly helping the spoil heap move down the mountain.

Culminating Activity (page 65)

The chart should include the following answers:

1. The story takes place in an isolated mountainous area near the Ohio River.

2. The story takes place in the 1960s. Hints are that M.C.'s parents met right after World War II, that M.C. sings the Beatles song "Ticket to Ride," and that the book was published in 1974.

3. The book is set in the summertime.

4. The weather is very hot and humid. There are evening thunderstorms and it is sometimes foggy.

5. The area is filled with mountains, hills, ridges, valleys, passes, and gullies. It includes a lake and the nearby Ohio River. The region is thick with trees and brush. Walking paths are sparse and steep.

6. The area has been affected by the arrival of strip miners, who have stripped the tops of the mountains to get to the coal underneath. The strip mining has left ugly patches through the hills, and is responsible for mounds of debris.

7. Outsiders struggle to find their way around the area, and to climb the steep paths.

8. The Higgins home sits beneath a pile of strip mining debris. This spoil heap is slowly sliding down the mountain.

Comprehension Assessment (pages 67–68)

1. A. follow

2. F. "'Wouldn't have hurt you,' he called."
   H. "The thought that Ben was nearby but unseen was all right with M.C."

3. C. Ben and M.C. trust each other, and work well together.

4. E. "Ben knows what I'm doing almost as soon as I do."

5. D. Friendship can rise above fear and prejudice.

6. F. M.C. stands up to his father, saying that Ben is his friend.

7. For just a moment, Jones lets go of the defensiveness and arrogance that cloud his personality. He appears to accept, and even appreciate, that his son is becoming his own man. This may be a sign that, in the future, Jones will be less competitive and aggressive with M.C. Perhaps now he can start to see his son as a young man, not a boy. Perhaps he will respect M.C. and listen to him, rather than shutting him out.

8. A. "For an instant his eyes were full of pride."